100 Things For Toddler
Coloring Book

Published May 2017

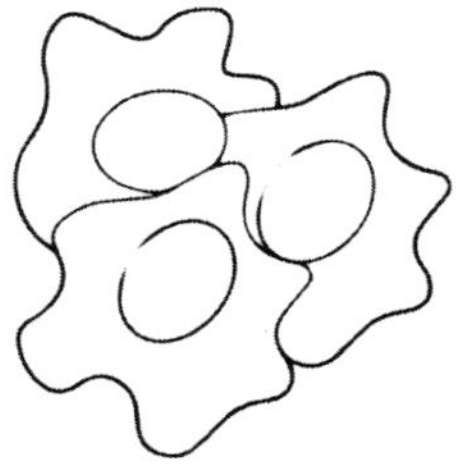

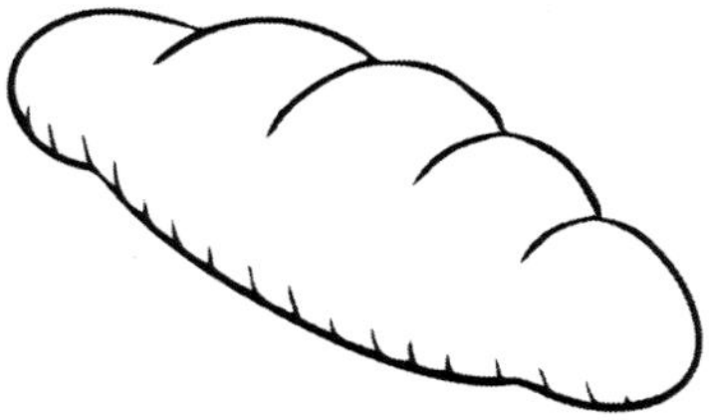

100 THINGS

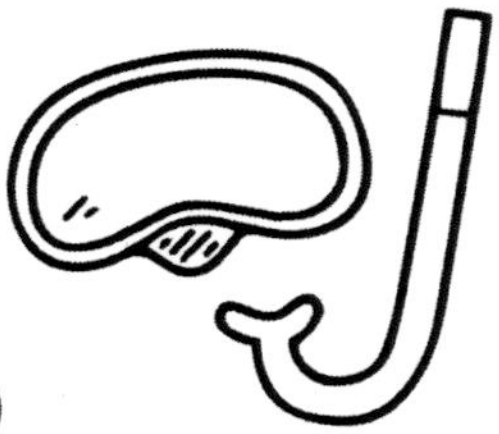

FOR TODDLER

COLORING BOOK

Belongs To . . . .

TEST YOUR COLORS

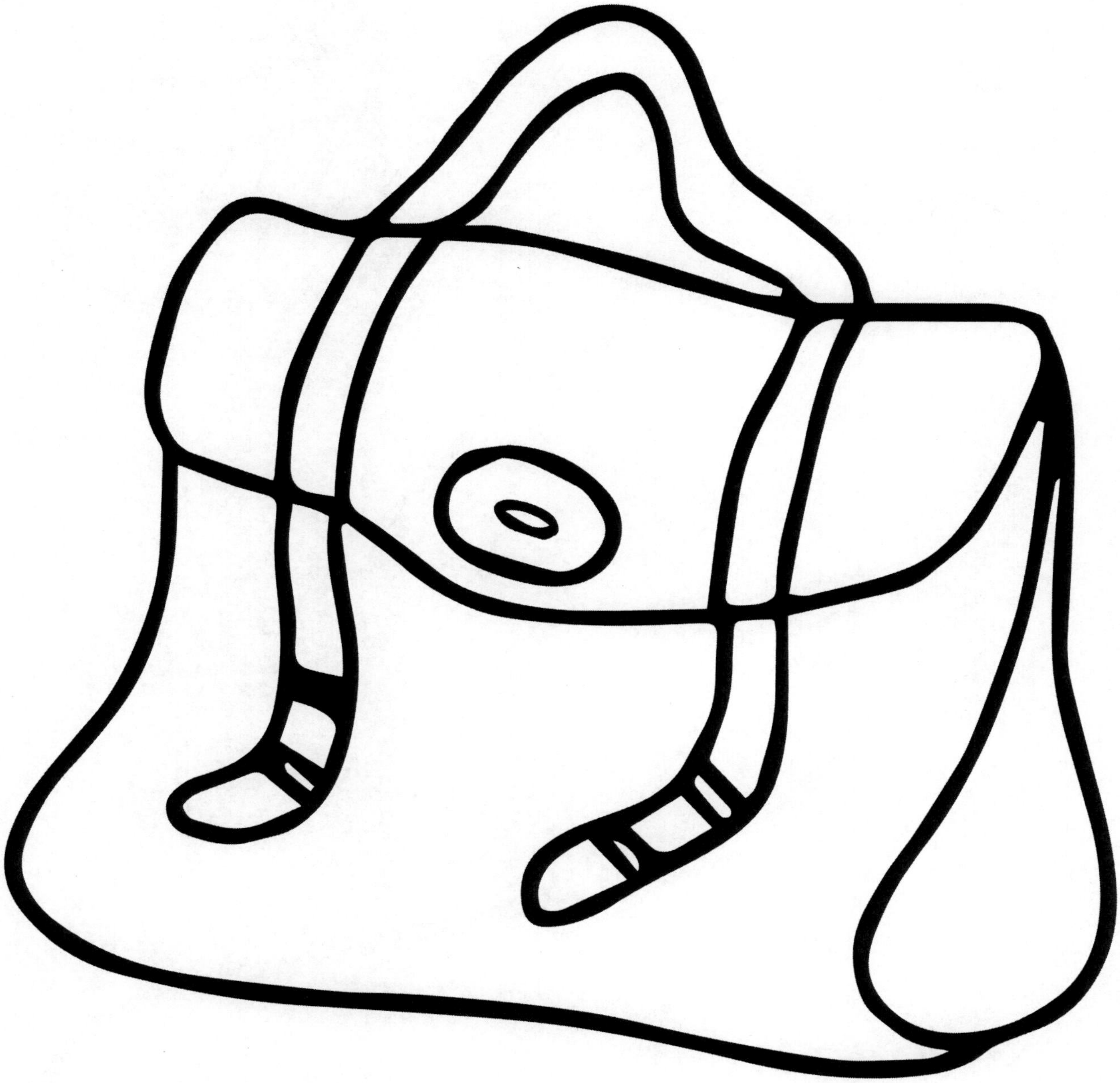

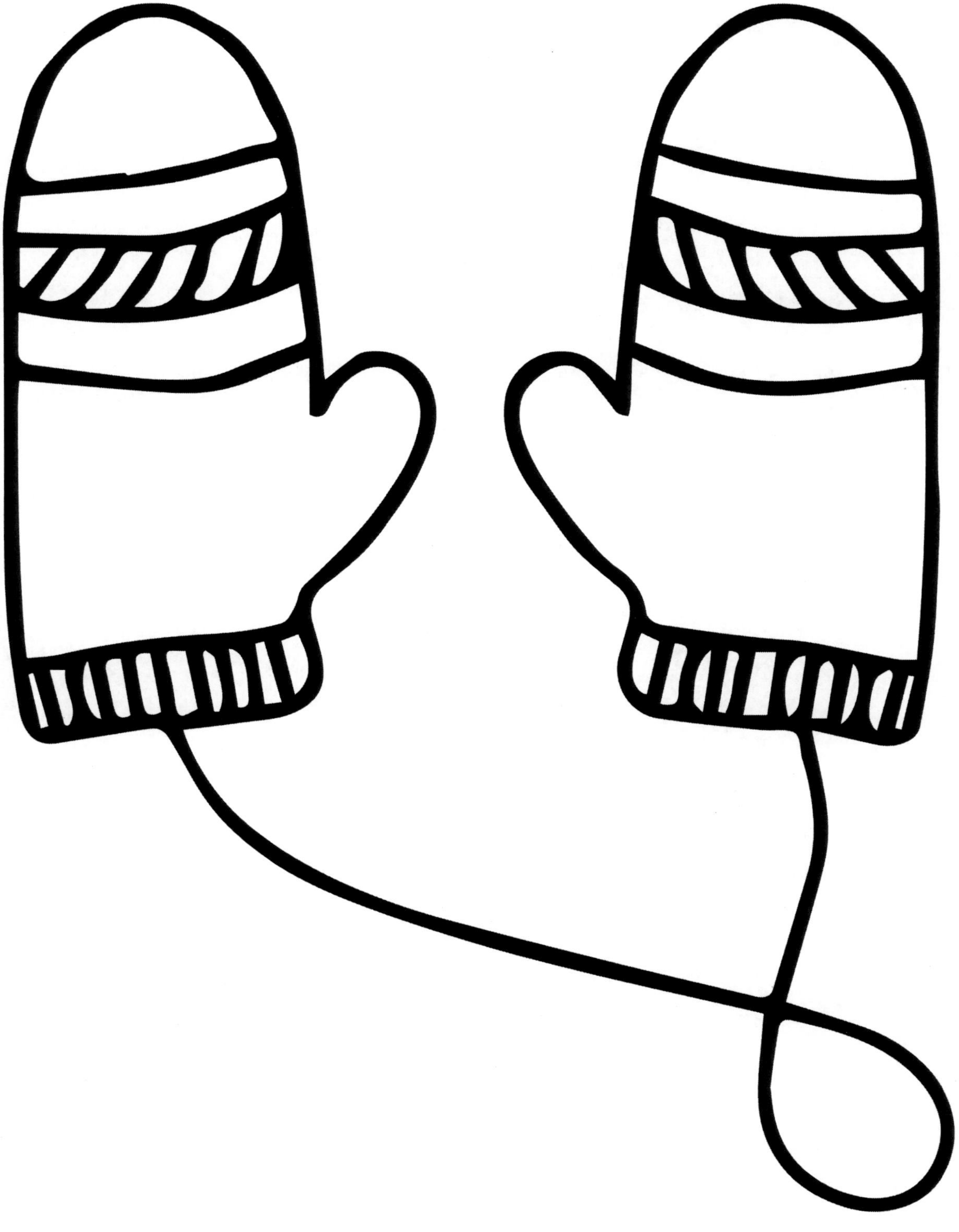

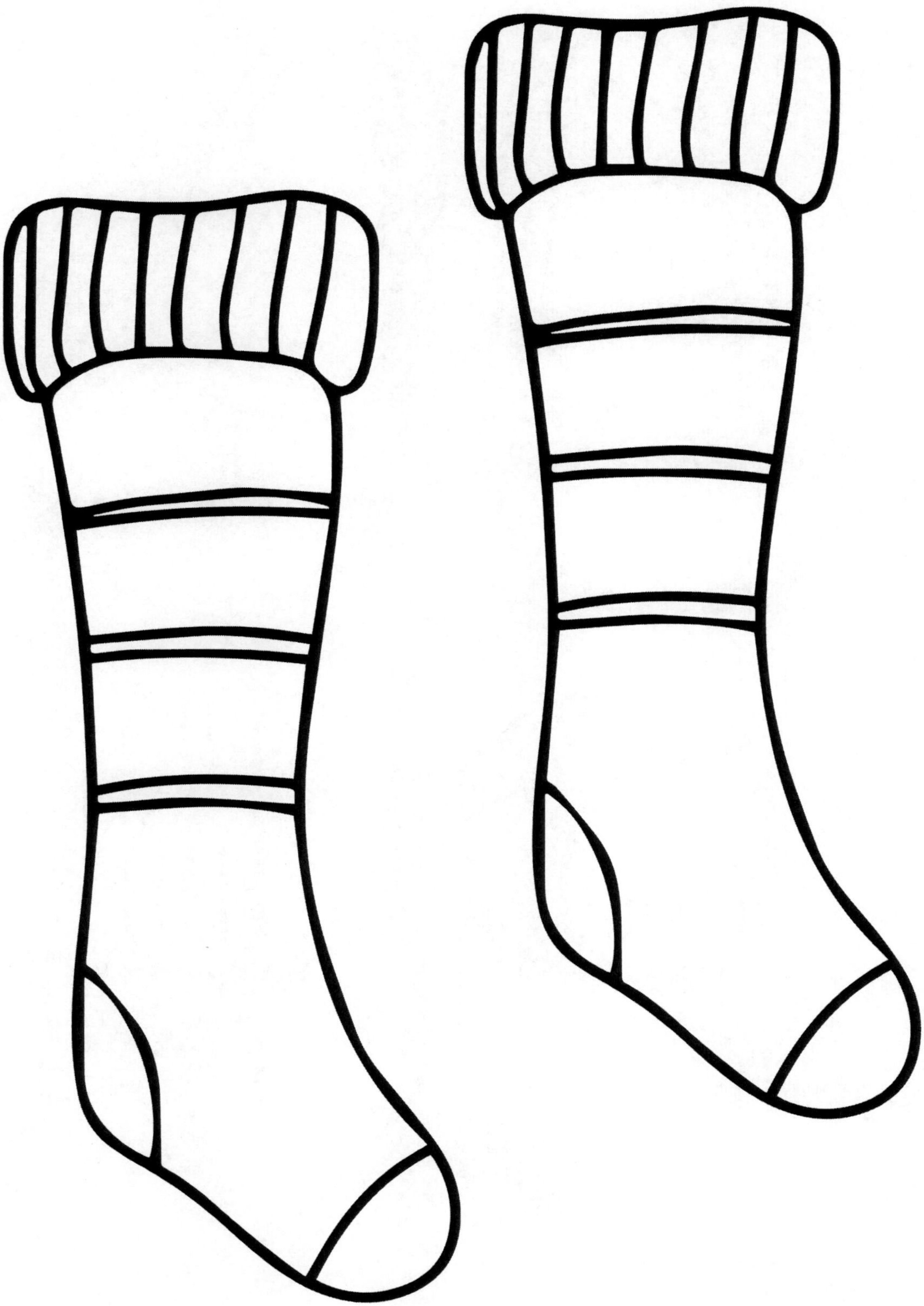

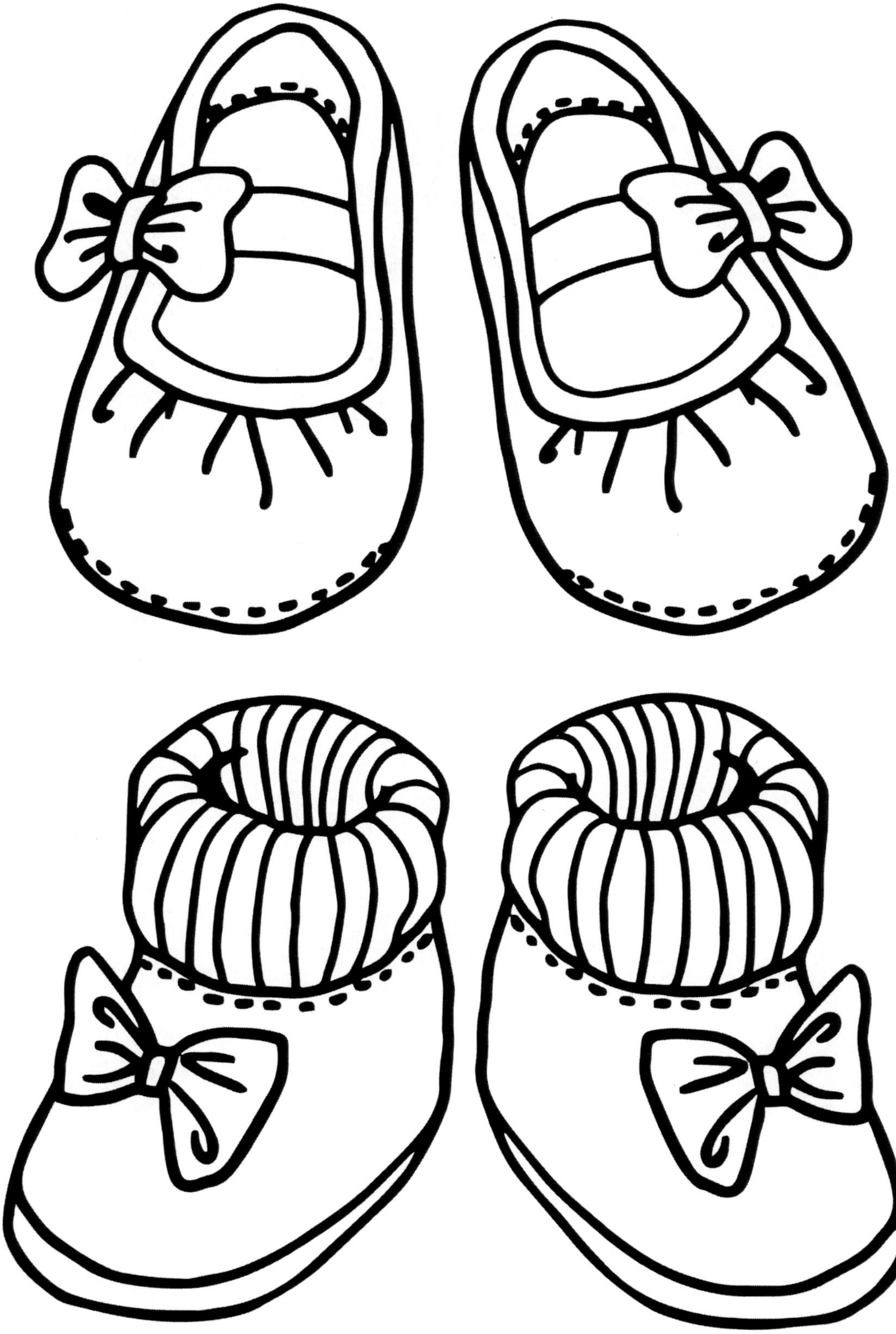

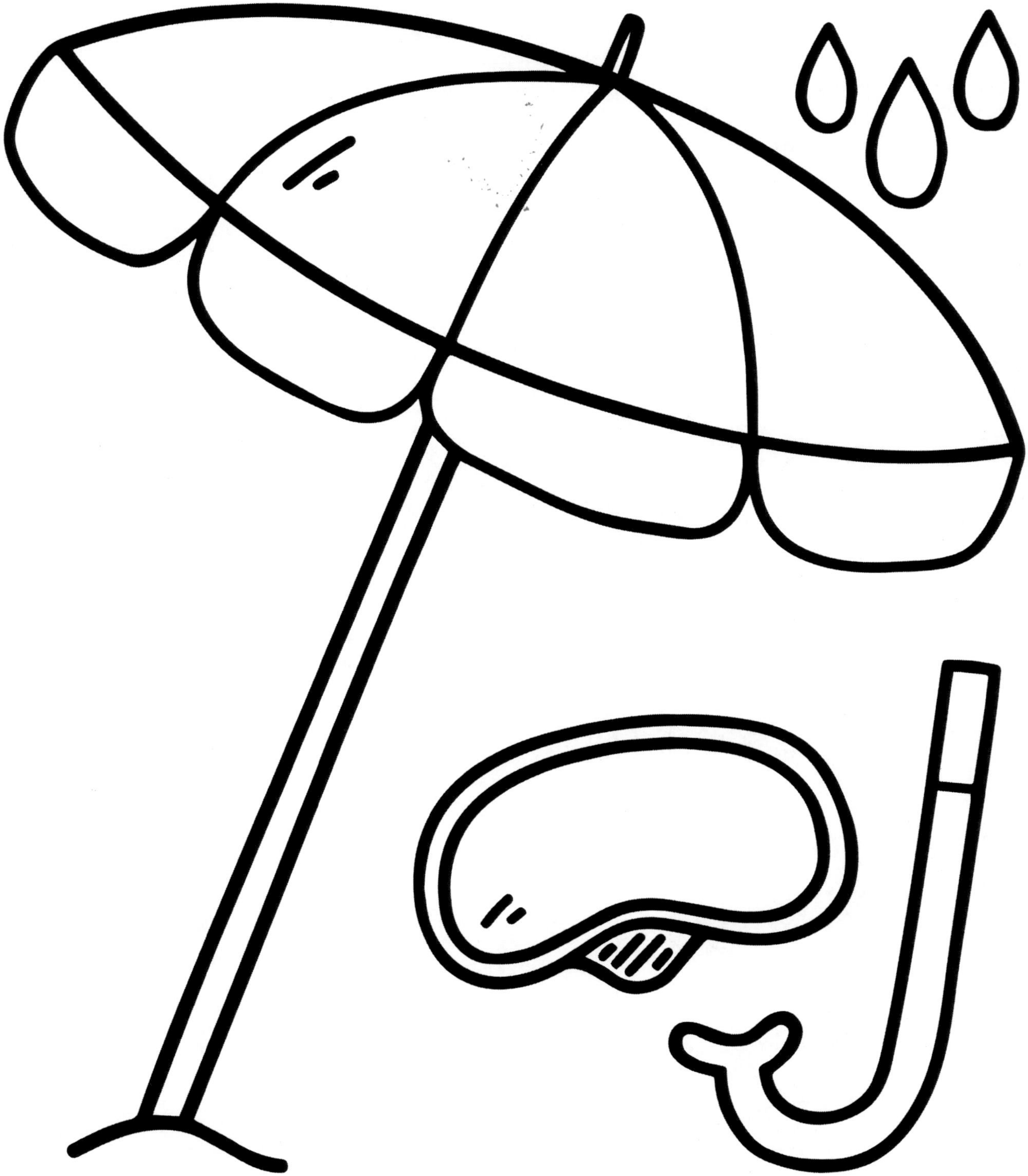

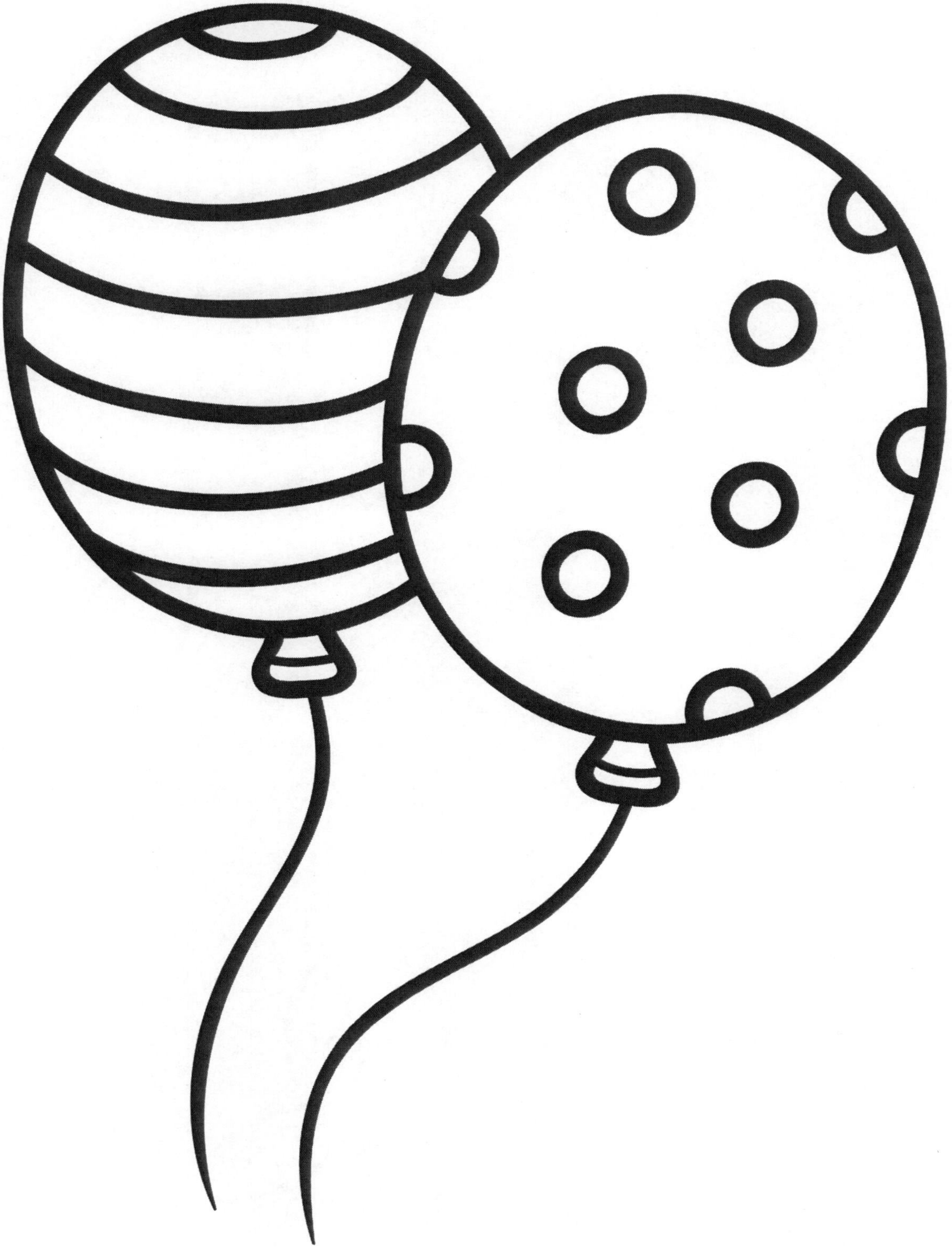

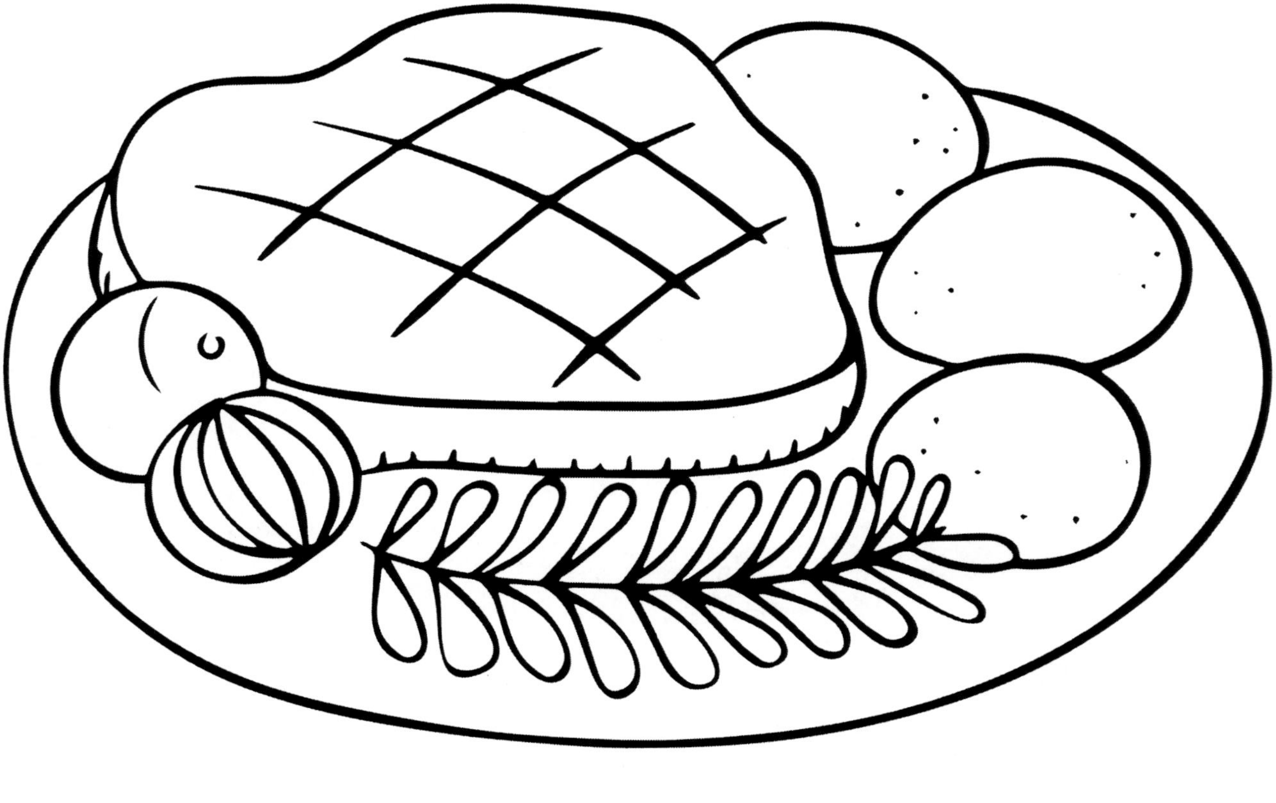

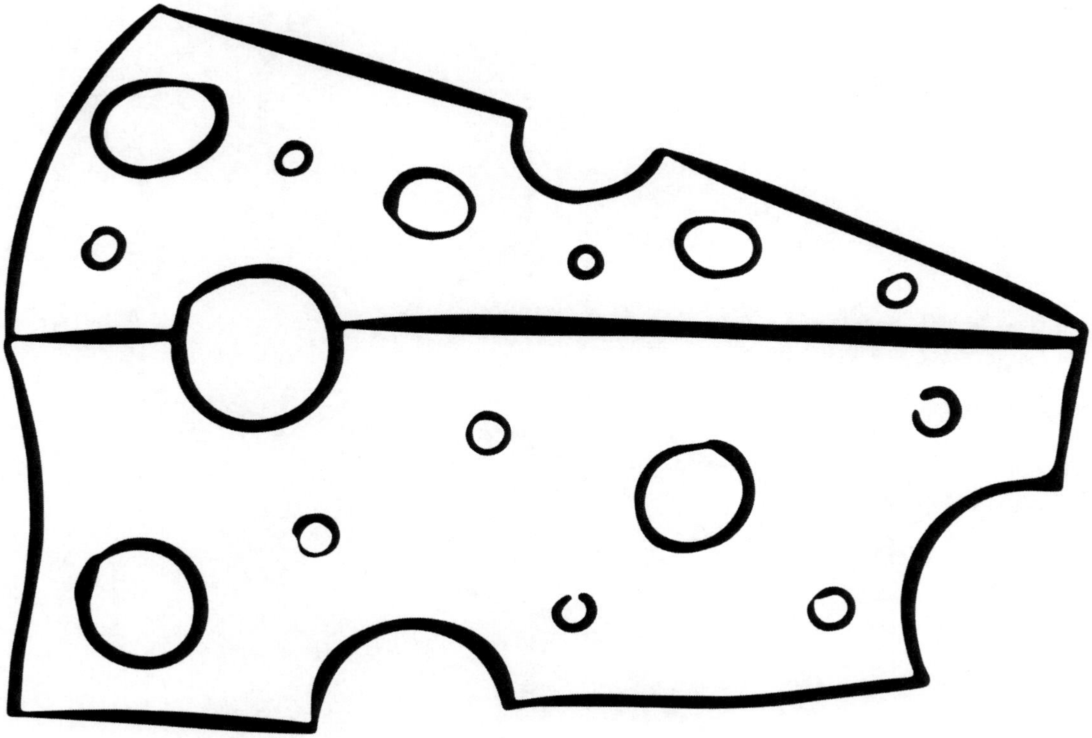

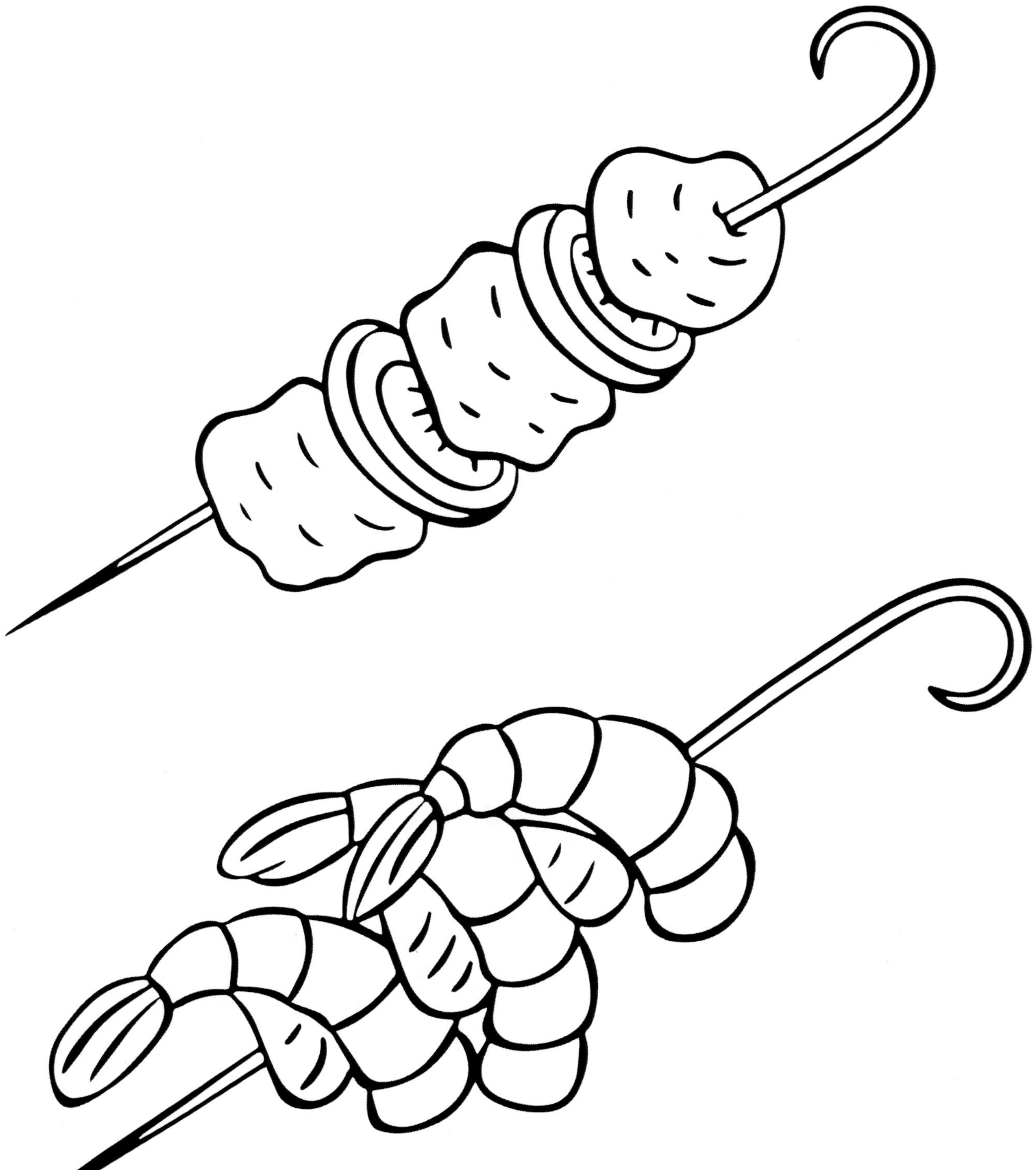

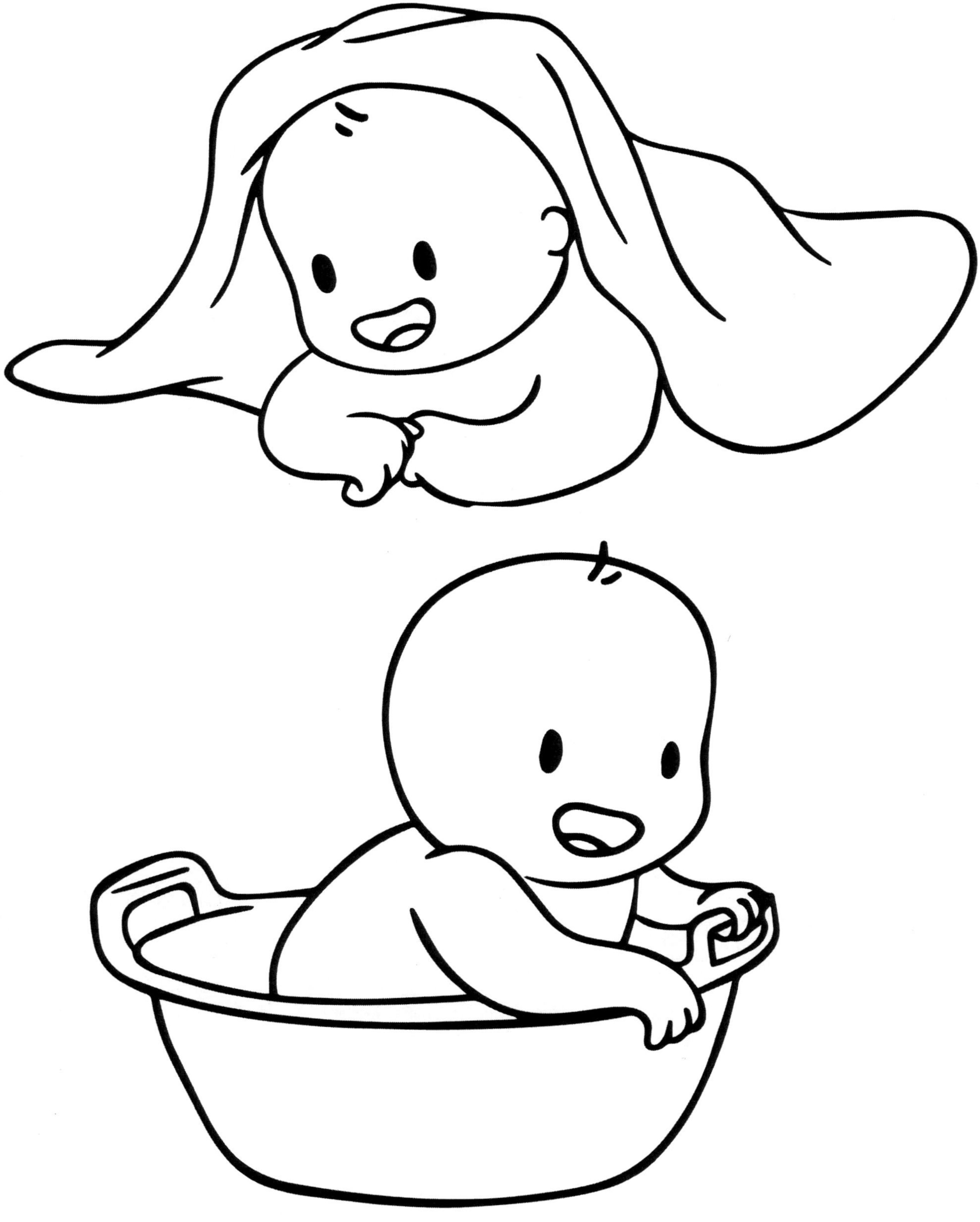

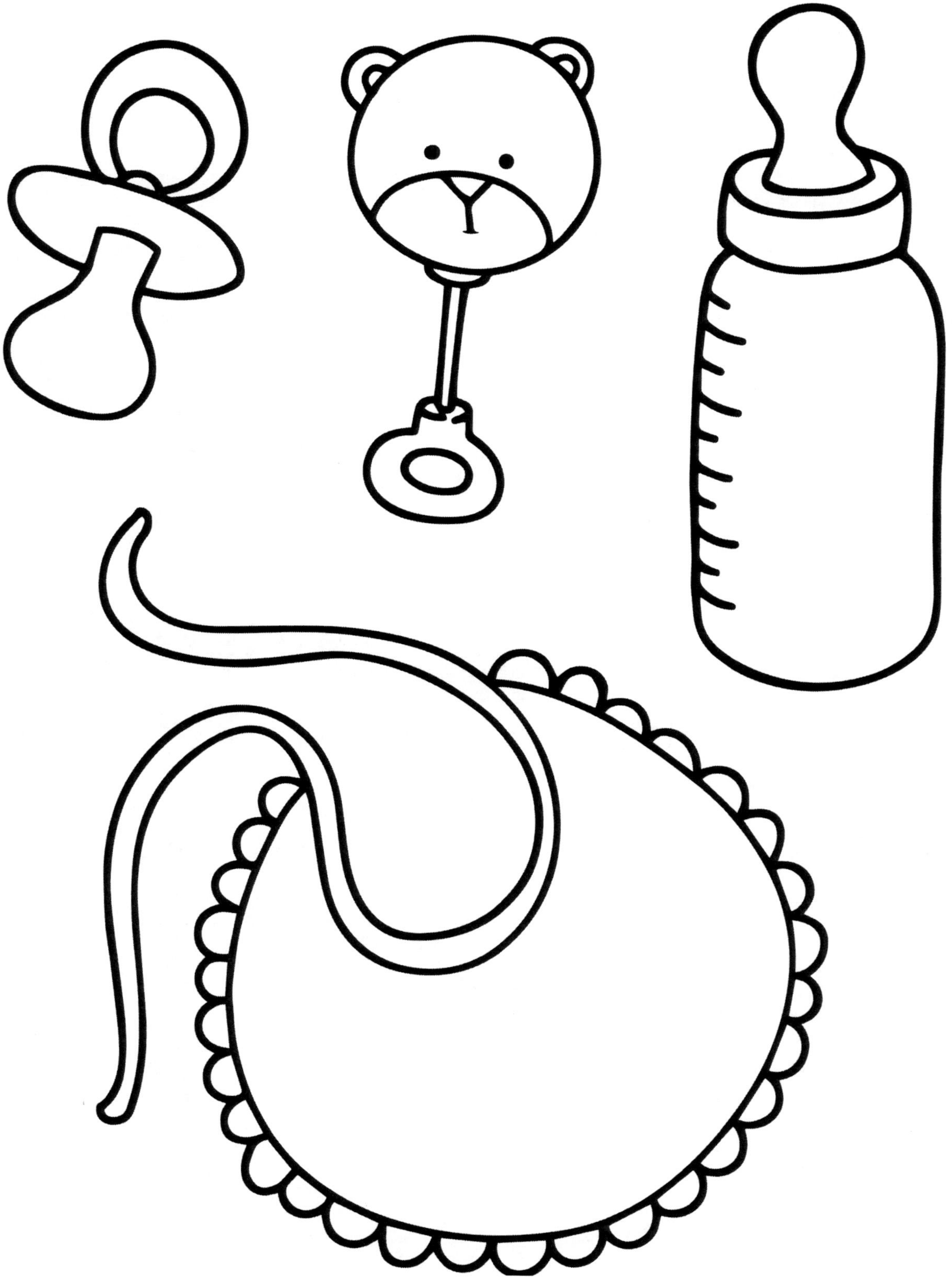

C
B
A

THANK YOU

Made in United States
North Haven, CT
01 June 2023

37232241R00057